PLUMB LINES

JERRY MANNERY

PRESS

www.xulonpress.com

Plumb Lines

A collection of poems, prose, proverbs and paintings
to glorify and extol the Lord and to enlighten,
encourage and edify the readers

Foreward

Several decades ago and barely out of our teens, the writer of this literary work and I, forged a collaborative creative friendship based on mutual respect and admiration. He shared with me many of his literary interest and poetry. I shared with him my fragment song ideas and fledgling guitar skills. In the very beginning and during various social gatherings, Jerry would introduce himself as a "writer" when asked the question, "What do you do?" Back then it was amusing to me because neither one of us had published anything – not even close – not yet. I would barely call myself a musician but Jerry seemed to have a confidence and knowing that writing would be part of his life's work. Little did I know that my collaboration with him would be that of a witness to a young man's amazing life journey of what behavioral psychologists call a "self-fulfilling prophecy."

Unlike the legend of the Mississippi blues man going down to the crossroads to make a pact with the devil, I witnessed a young man turn from the alluring temptations of the world toward the Word of God for insight and inspiration for righteous living. Jerry was such a stickler for doing what was right that on one particular occasion he wouldn't let me throw out an apple core that I'd been munching on as we traveled down the highway. I called it feeding the bugs and birds; he called it being a litterbug!

I was a witness, thirty seven years ago (as his best man) when he and his beautiful wife, Sharon, stood before God, family and friends, on one of the most gorgeous crisp blue sky days one could imagine - to say their vows in holy matrimony at the home of his older brother Herman.

I witnessed his becoming a father, first to baby Yanci and then to baby Jerron and marveled at his dedication to his wife and children and his determination to give them stability and raise them in a Christian home. I remember the privilege of visiting them during my business travels and being at the breakfast table laughing at and with the family as the kids laughed at me for loving Fruit Loops.

I witnessed how he entered the gospel music industry as the assistant to one of the great gospel legends, Frank Williams and how this resulted in his opportunity to be an award winning gospel songwriter, music industry executive, executive producer and Executive Director of The Mississippi Mass Choir respectively.

I witnessed his working two jobs (maybe three!) with long hours allowing his wife the option to be a stay at home mom.

It was during his dual responsibility as a Firefighter/EMT (Emergency Medical Technician) that inspired his rendering of the hauntingly moving piece "When You Get Old", from composite encounters with the elderly in crisis.

I am witness to the fact that the author honorably served his country first as a veteran of the United States Navy, but then later, and later as we served together in the 134th Combat Support Hospital of the Mississippi Army Reserves and National Guard. Double duty!

I witnessed him volunteering his time, talents and treasure by working in his church.

I witnessed him actively express faith, hope and support to his extended family, friends, co-workers and community during times of trials and challenge – with the greatest of these expressions being love.

I witnessed his obedience to the Holy Spirit as he accepted the call of ordination as a minister of the gospel and witnessed him preach his first sermon – "Your Bus Is On Fire." That then said...I've witnessed many amazing things in this man's life.

I share about Jerry's achievements as a witness to someone who chose the high road. Most of us have respect for those who "walk the talk" and Jerry's life exemplifies both. My feelings of respect for and about this writer are even stronger today because I have witnessed him live such an amazing life of integrity.

Before I read this work, I paid no attention to the term *plumb line* during my studying and reading of the Bible. I've read the Bible at least three times cover to cover and this phrase never stuck. Jerry Mannery has brought to light an obscure but powerful action noun for us to meditate upon, for this age and for ages to come. This work challenges us to reexamine ourselves with a humble heart and the finest of measurement. This work challenges us to examine our motives, intentions, attitudes, thoughts, heart and soul. Jerry also challenges us to be guided by the Word and the truth of scripture which exhorts us to, "be ye ever perfect even as your Father in heaven" - a *plumb line*.

It would behoove all of us to read and heed this work and take a note from the prophet Amos. "And the Lord asked me, "What do you see Amos?" "A Plumb Line" I replied. Then the Lord said "Look, I am setting a plumb line among my people Israel. (Amos 7:8)

I hope that each reader of this book will be as deeply touched within his or her heart and soul as I've been throughout the years as a witness to this author's creative life...Selah.

Rev. Dr. James V. Steele

Preface

*A*fter reading the parable of the Talents, at the age of twenty-three, I asked God to reveal the talent(s) meant for me. Almost immediately I felt the need to write. I knew that one must "study to showeth thyself approved unto God, a workman that needeth not to be ashamed, rightly dividing the word of truth." (2 Timothy 2:15) So I returned to school at Jackson State University, Jackson, Mississippi and majored in English literature, with minors in journalism and mass communication.

There I met my mentor Dr. Margaret Walker Alexander - noted author of *Jubilee* and *For My People*. It was there that I was blessed to share my writings with her and to receive invaluable constructive criticism and encouragement. It was from her that I learned that "writing was 10 percent inspiration and 90 percent perspiration."

Some of the "message seeds" I was given have sat dormant for thirty-plus years in journals, legal pads, word documents and scraps of all sort of paper. After sharing a few of them with my dear friend and brother George Stewart, he reminded me that the "graveyard is the richest place on earth; full of treasures in earthen vessel, and if I did not sow these "message seeds" soon that I would inadvertently add to the cemetery's vast estate." His words became a tipping point for *Plumb Lines*.

> Every word and line,
> Is rather by design,
> To suggest than to teach,
> To whisper than to speak…

Jerry Mannery

I Thank My God Every Time I Remember You

"A man who finds a wife finds a good thing and obtains favor from the Lord".
-Proverbs 18:22, HCSB

Sharon B. Mannery

"Like arrows in the hand of a warrior, so are the children of one's youth.
How blessed is the man whose quiver is full of them." -Psalms 127:4-5, NASB

Yanci Mannery-Baker (Benjamin), Jerron Eli Mannery (Kassundra)
(My Children)
Kennedi Mannery, Landon Mannery, Ansleigh Mannery and Olivia
Baker (My grandchildren)
Valerie Blue (My god-daughter)

"Honor your mother and your father, as the Lord your God has commanded you, so that you
may live long and that it may go well with you in the land the Lord your God is giving you.
-Deuteronomy 5:16, NIV

Beatrice Johnson-Mannery*, Jalatherous Mannery (My parents)
Eli Johnson*, Ada Johnson* (My grandparents)
Joe Thurman*, Lela Thurman* (My in-laws)

"If either of them falls down, one can help the other up. But pity anyone who falls and has
no one to help them up." -Ecclesiastes 4:10, NIV

Mildred Wilson*, Doris Jones, Herman Mannery, Larry Mannery,
Steve Mannery, Deborah Clayton, Patricia Mannery, Lisa McDonald,
and Gregory Johnson (My siblings)
Betty Williams, Helen Blue* (My sisters in law)
Harold Johnson* (My cousin/brother)
All of my nieces, nephews and cousins, both Johnson, Mannery,
and Blue

"Not giving up meeting together, as some are in the habit of doing, but encouraging one
another– and all the more as you see the Day approaching." -Hebrew 10:25, NIV

Anderson United Methodist Church (Pastor Joe May, Jackson,
Mississippi), More Than Conquerors Faith Church (Pastor
Steve Green, Birmingham, Alabama), Mississippi Mass Choir
Ministries, Inc. (Executive board and members)

I Thank My God Every Time I Remember You

"One who has unreliable friends soon comes to ruin, but there is a friend who sticks closer than a brother." -Proverbs 18:24, NIV

Frank Williams*, Elder Benjamin Cone Jr.*, Hoyett Owens, Betty Owens, James V. Steele, George Stewart, Jerry Smith, Stan Jones, Marvin Hicks, Sylvester Mims, Zac Harmon, Bishop Jeffery Stallworth, Bishop Andrew Ford, Frederick Knight, Rev. Samuel Wansley, Rev. Milton Biggham, Katrina Williams, Roy Wooten*, Chip Davis, M. Thurston Cox*, James Mitchell, Luis Manjarres, Valerie Wilson, Rev. Samuel L. Thompson, Rev. Stephen F. Mason, Rev. Haran Griffin, Rev. Jim Holley, Norma Cannon, Attorney Karl Washington, Pastor Mike Smith

"We think in pictures even though we speak and write with words."

Tracy Applewhite (Illustrator)

"As iron sharpens iron, so one person sharpens another." -Proverbs 27:17, NIV

John Milton Wesley (Editor)

"The gift of a man maketh room for him, and before the great it leadeth him." -Proverb 18:16, YLT

Malaco Music Group (Tommy Couch Sr., Tommy Couch Jr., Wolf Stephenson, Stewart Madison, Rosetta Anderson and Staff) Faith-Based Communications Inc. team members, TV One (Cathy Hughes), Dr. Bobby Jones, Dorothy Norwood, Don Jackson, Dr. David Molapo and Mamikie Molapo, McDonald's AACM (Marty Gillis, Harry Smith, Marc O'Ferrell), Jackson Fire Department, Xulon Publishing, Gospel Music Community, Anyone I overlooked

"For whosoever shall do the will of my Father which is in heaven, the same is my brother, and sister and mother." -Matthew 12:50, KJV

Brothers and sisters in Christ

"Remember those who led you, who spoke the word of God to you; and considering the result of their conduct, imitate their faith." -Hebrews 13:7, NASB

Margaret-Walker Alexander*

"I have planted, Apollos watered; but God gave the increase." -1 Corinthians 3:6, KJB

"To God be the glory for the great things He has done!"

*In Memoriam

Table of Contents

Table of Contents

by Jerry Mannery

How These Pages
Were Stained

The hand of the Lord

Was upon me,

It was too wonderful

To contain,

My cup soon overflowed,

And with words

These pages were stained.

Echoing

When I speak of God,

I'm like an underground spring

Far beneath the surface,

At my best; just echoing

Some most marvelous things

A bubbling brook spoke to me,

A river told it an ocean overheard,

All about the Fathomless Sea.

Otherwise, you'll have to take my word for it.

O MY GOD!

When I consider the works of Your hands,
All that the universe has on display,
And hear the heavens declaring Your Glory,
My soul spontaneously says,

"O my God!
How Glorious You are!
O my God!
Of You I am in awe!
Of Your mercies, might and majesty!
"O my God!

When I read in Your Holy Word,
How You spoke to the land and sea,
And from them came forth fish and birds;
But to Yourself You spoke and created me.

O my God!

Your knowledge is high above me,
Far too wonderful to know,
Way beyond my reach and speech,
I bow, believe and adore.

Just to write one word about You,
Would take the seven seas,
The ink would fail me,
The pen emptied completely.

O my God…O my God…O my God!
My soul cries out,
O my God!

Scriptural reference: Psalm 8:3

The Lord is my shepherd; I shall not want. He maketh me to lie down in green pastures: he leadeth me beside the still waters. He restoreth my soul: he leadeth

Psalm 23 And Me

I Am is my shepherd,
And I am His sheep,
Deaf, dumb and blind to the world,
In green pastures I deeply sleep.

His omnipotent rod comforts,
Accounts and corrects.
His animate and angelic staff,
Supports, sustains and protects.

The shadow of a serpent doesn't sting,
The shadow of a sword doesn't kill,
Nor does Death Valley's shadow,
So I have no fear, and will not veer or stand still.

My body and mind are connected,
When bad news beats at my door.
I will not lose sleep; He's preparing a feast!
Then leaves goodness and mercy behind and goes forth.

Scriptural reference: Psalm 23

Sea of Forgiveness and Forgetfulness

My accusers raised their hands,
Readied them to cast their stones,
Raised them on the witness stand,
Testified about my wrongs.

Jesus raised his hand,
On a hill called Calvary.
He took their stones and my wrongs,
And cast them into the sea.

He cast them into the sea,
Of grace, love and mercy.
The sea of forgiveness and forgetfulness,
To never again accuse me.

He blotted out my transgressions,
Every trace, scent and memory.
Accepted my repentance,
And from guilt, he set me free.

Into the deep, dark, distant depths,
Far from the furthermost shore,
With no trespassing on my trespasses,
Now they rest on the sea floor.

As the heavens are high above the earth,
So are His grace, love and mercy.
He showered me with unmerited favor,
And cast my sins into the sea.

My face bares no mark of my shame,
My heart hides my regrets.
Only He could restore my good name,
For He forgives and forgets.

Scriptural reference: Micah 7:19 / Jeremiah 31:34

He cast them into the sea

Of grace, love and mercy.

The sea of forgiveness and forgetfulness,

To never again accuse me.

forgiven and forgotten

Prodigal Train

Once I was a prodigal train,
My life completely off track.
If not for my Engineer's grace,
I would not have made it back.

Pushed by a head of steam,
I jumped the straight and narrow track.
Demanded my portion and lot,
Gathered it, and never looked back.

I chased runaway trains,
Wasted fuel up my stack.
Famine fell on me like acid rain,
What I had became things I lacked.

My boiler had never been so empty,
For unnatural things I hungered and thirsted.
The green grass over the fence
Had now become Astroturf.

I became a derailed prodigal-train,
Received temporal lift by carnal jacks.
My load proved too great a strain,
I was back on my back.

Off the rails between heaven and hell,
Lost and alone in a dark and distant land,
This locomotive almost became a "loco-motive,"
Off the Author and Finisher's plan.

At the bottom I came to my senses,
And remembered the one and only crane
That can uplift, re-track and restore
A derailed prodigal train.

Not worthy to call His name,
But glory be to the Lord.
Thanks to Christ, the only Crane,
I am back in the train yard!

Scriptural reference: Luke 15:11

Once I was a
    prodigal train,
My life completely
    off track.
If not for my
    Engineer's grace,
I would not have
    made it back.

Miranda Rights for Sinners

You have the right to remain silent,
But you have no reason to,
For nothing that you confess
Can be used against you,

When we confess our sins,
God is faithful and just.
He forgives us and He cleanses us
With the blood of Jesus.

We cannot afford an attorney,
Jesus represents you and me.
He is the only advocate we need
For the court to set us free.

Scriptural reference: 1 John 1:9

1 John 1:9

If... When one thing happens, the other is a guarantee

We... All have sinned, and fallen short of His glory

Confess...To admit; call it what God calls it

Our sins...What grieves God in words, thoughts and deeds

God is Faithful... He can be depended upon

And just... Respecter of none

To forgive us our sins... Pardoning

And cleanse us from all unrighteousness... Is reconciling.

Scriptural reference: 1 John 1:9

Jesus Got Me Off

Once I was held in the sinners' jail,
But Jesus got me off.
He became my lawyer and paid my bail;
Otherwise I could not pay the cost.

The prosecutor had all the facts,
But Jesus got me off.
I was even caught in the very act,
But Jesus paid the cost.

By Moses's Law he issued a demand,
But Jesus got me off.
That I receive the wages of a sinner man,
But Jesus paid the cost.

The verdict was in before I took the stand,
Because Jesus got me off.
Jurors had stones in their hearts and hands,
But Jesus paid the cost.

Just knew my life would soon be gone,
But Jesus got me off.
So I prepared myself to be stoned,
But Jesus paid the cost.

He told the sinless to "cast the first stone,"
When Jesus got me off.
One by one all my accusers went home,
Because Jesus had paid the cost.

The verdict was no condemnation,
Because Jesus got me off.
He told me to now "go and sin no more."
Jesus has paid the cost.

Scriptural reference: John 8:1-11

Justified

(Just If I'd Never Sinned)

Justified…
Just if I'd never sinned,
Old things are passed away,
All is new again.

Justified…
Just if I'd always been,
Perfect in His sight,
And all is new again.

Once the blood was applied,
The cleansing blood of Christ,
I was washed and made whole;
I am pure in His eyes.

Just if I'd never been charged,
As if we'd never been torn apart,
As if I'd never fallen short of His glory,
He gave me a brand new heart.

Because of His perfect love,
His perfect sacrifice,
My death sentence was changed,
To eternal life.

My sins were charged to Him,
And his righteousness to me,
He removed them as far away,
As the west is from the east.

Scriptural reference: Romans 5:1

jus ·ti ·fied
ˈjəstəˌfīd/
adjective/past tense verb

Justified is the act of God declaring one righteous and not guilty of sin in His sight.

It is the same as when a judge declares in a court of law that a defendant is not guilty, and all charges are dropped, after which the record is expunged. In the "eyesight of the court" it's "just if" the person was never charged.

It operates the same way in the Court of Grace. When God forgives our sins, through the advocacy of Jesus Christ, the charges are dropped and our records are wiped clean. Although we are not innocent, we are declared not guilty. Not right, yet not held in the wrong. Not without shame, yet without blame. All made known, yet regarded as unknown. In the "eyesight of Grace," we are "Justified... Just As If" we had never sinned.

He is the only way,

The truth and the life,

No one comes to the Father,

Except through Jesus Christ.

Only One Way Home

Only one way,
Only one way home.
And it is through Jesus,
Jesus Christ alone.

He is the only way,
The truth and the life;
No one comes to the Father
Except through Jesus Christ.

Although it has been said,
"All roads lead to Rome."
But to the house of many mansions,
There is but one way home.

All other paths you take,
That you seek or may find,
Will only lead you astray,
Like the blind leading the blind.

There is "no other name under heaven
By which we can be saved."
Only the name of Jesus
Can free this captured slave.

Only one way home,
To the homeland of the soul.
To live forevermore
In that heavenly household.

Only one way home.
And it is through Christ alone.
He is the only way,
Our sins to atone.

Scriptural reference: John 14:6

Don't "Be-fitting" Me Anymore

When I laid my all on the altar,
God altered me from within.
Like a tailor He let me out in places,
In others, He had to take me in.

Now things that use to "be-fit" me,
Don't "be-fitting" me anymore.
Things I use to do and say,
Are left with no allure.

After putting on His righteousness,
I can't fit into forms of godlessness.
My thoughts, words, will and deeds
Now match His divine code of dress.

Now wearing the belt of truth,
My old wardrobe would clash;
Lying, cheating, deception and ruse
Have all been thrown in the trash.

Now I walk in the newness of life;
It's perfect shoes on my feet
That keeps me walking worthy of Christ,
Clad in His Gospel, readiness and peace.

All that hinders has been laid aside,
And with endurance I run the race.
My eyes firmly fixed on Christ,
The Author and Finisher of my faith.

There's been a change in my life;
I am not the same as before,
Now things that use to "be-fit" me
Don't "be-fitting" me anymore.

Scriptural reference: Ephesian 6: 14-15

Praying Grandma

I had a praying Grandma;
Her only weakness was bad knees,
The result of staying down on them
Fervently praying for the family.

If anyone could get one through,
Grandma "shonuff" got her share.
I wouldn't be standing here today
Had it not been for her prayers.

I used to hear her in the midnight hour,
Way before the break of dawn,
Talking to God like she was His friend,
Saying, "Lord keep 'em from hurt and harm."

Heard her say, "Lord send your angels,
And if it's not too much, send a pair,
Send goodness and mercy to walk with them.
Have grace to meet them there.

Father, please forgive them,
Charge their head and not their heart.
I trained them up in the way they should go;
When they are old, let them not depart.

Grandma is now gone
To that mansion in the sky,
But as long as I live,
Grandma's prayers will never die.

Scriptural reference: James 5:16

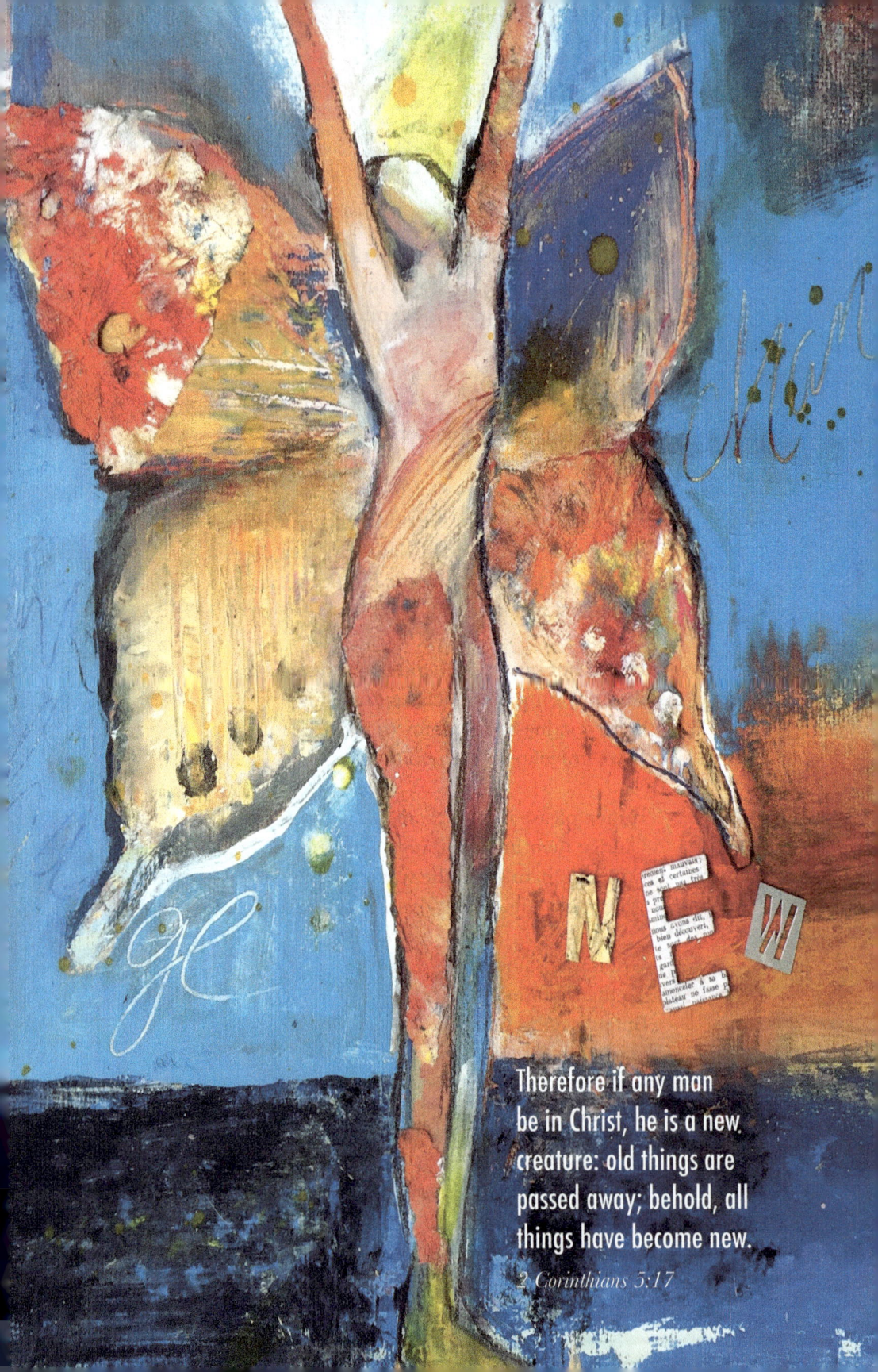

Therefore if any man be in Christ, he is a new creature: old things are passed away; behold, all things have become new.

2 Corinthians 5:17

Butterfly's Praise

Once I was a caterpillar;
Now I'm a butterfly.
I've been transformed, been re-born,
And Jesus is the reason why,

No re-entering my mother's womb
And I didn't have to die;
I've been transformed, been re-born,
And Jesus is the reason why.

Once I lifted Him up,
A miracle happened inside of me.
Like "The People Could Fly,"
I was lifted off of my feet.

Some ask, "How could this be?"
When they see me soaring high.
"How could he become a new creature?"
And this was my reply.

Once I was a caterpillar;
Now I'm a butterfly.
I've been transformed, been re-born,
And Jesus is the reason why.

Scriptural reference: 2 Corinthians 5:17

BEA'S RECIPE:
GERMAN CHOCOLATE CAKE

Cake
- 3/4 c all-purpose flour
- 2 tsp baking powder
- 1 tsp fine sea salt
- 1 c unsweetened shredded coconut
- 3/4 c sugar
- 1/2 c unsalted butter (room temp)
- 2 tsp packed grated orange peel
- 2 large eggs
- 1 tsp vanilla extract

- 1 cup canned unsweetened coconut milk
- 6 oz bittersweet choc. broken into 1/2 inch chunks divided
- 1/2 cup sweetened flaked coconut

Coconut Drizzle (Yum!)
- 3/4 cup powdered sugar
- 2 tbsp (or more) coconut milk
- 1/2 tsp vanilla extract
VANILLA ICE CREAM!

BUTTERMILK

BAKING SPICE

MORTON SALT

HMMMMM ?

WORKING TOGETHER FOR MY GOOD

"And we know that all things work together for good to them that love God, to them who are the called according to his purpose."
(Roman 8:28, KJV)

Although all things are not good, they work together for good to them that love God, to them who are called according to His purpose.

As a young boy this Scripture came to life for me as I watched my mother, Beatrice Johnson, prepare to bake her famous German Chocolate Cake. The first thing she did was gather *all* of the ingredients and place them on the kitchen table: Martha White all-purpose flour, German semi-sweet chocolate, Borden's buttermilk, eggs from the family's chickens, McCormick pure vanilla extract, Morton iodized salt, Domino sugar, Clabber Girl baking powder, Pillsbury flaked coconuts, and pecans from a tree up the street.

I figured since her cake tasted so good, surely the individual ingredients would as well. "Bea," – as my siblings and I affectionately called her- "can I taste some of the cake stuff on the counter?" "No", she said, "wait 'til it's done." After whining for a few minutes and her threatening to 'give me something to whine about,' she conceded and said, "Go ahead and taste them." And here's what happened….

Continued...

BEATRICE JOHNSON'S GERMAN CHOCOLATE CAKE

The first thing I tasted was the flour,
But it was dry and bland on its own.
No one told me buttermilk was sour;
I would not have tried it had I known.

The baking powder and butter were no better;
I could have left them on the table.
The semi-sweet chocolate was bitter;
I was fooled by the smell of the vanilla flavor.

I asked her why these ingredients
Didn't taste like her German chocolate cake,
She said "Wait 'til I mix them together,
And the stove is given time to bake."

As soon as the batter began to rise,
I reached for the hot oven door.
She said, "If you open it, don't be surprised
When the cake sinks to rise no more.

I set the oven's temperature and timer;
In the fullness of time they would tell.
You can't judge on how it looks
Or how you think it smells.

I pierced its center with a toothpick;
It's done if it comes out clean.
It still needs time to cool
For the pecan-coconut icing."

Cooling seemed to take forever,
But yes, it was worth the wait.
Now I know "all things work together,
For good to them who love the Lord,"
And Beatrice Johnson's German chocolate cake.

Scriptural reference: Roman 8:28

ALL THINGS

WORK TOGETHER FOR GOOD

Declaration of Dependence

I hereby declare these truths to be self-evident. I am totally, utterly, completely and unashamedly dependent upon God. I am incompetent in myself to claim anything of myself; my competence and sufficiency are from God. He has endowed me with eternal life, His spirit of liberty, and the pursuit of unspeakable joy. It is in Him that I live, move and have my being. All that is good and perfect and is heard or seen in me... is of Him... from Him...through Him... for Him...and to Him.

Jerry Mannery

Declaration of Dependence

I hereby declare these truths to be self-evident. I am totally, utterly, completely and unashamedly dependent upon God. I am incompetent in myself to claim anything of myself; my competence and sufficiency are from God. He has endowed me with eternal life, His spirit of liberty, and the pursuit of unspeakable joy. It is in Him that I live, move and have my being. All that is good and perfect and that is heard or seen in me…is of Him, from Him, through Him, for Him, and to Him. For…

Out of nothing, He created everything,
And He can just as easily
Return it from whence it came,
He need only say, "Let it be."
His knowledge is too high for me;
I cannot reach its door,
Not even its lowest step,
So I just bow, believe, and adore.

From the dust He formed me
And breathed life in my nose;
And if He withheld it,
My lungs will exhale to rise no more.
Every breath that I take,
Every beat of my heart,
Every step that I make
Is ordered by the Lord.

Naked into the world I came
And will surely leave here the same.
He gives and He takes away;
Blessed be His Holy name.
He proved His love for me
By giving His Son, Jesus Christ.
By His death my death sentence
Was changed to eternal life.

Continued…

His are the seeds I sow,
Others water with water from Him.
But He alone bid them grow,
And my cup to flow over the brim:
And He is the husbandman.
Jesus is the true vine;
From the root to the fruit,
From Him it is consigned.

By His grace, I'm saved through faith,
Amazingly sufficient for my thorns;
His mercy is new and everlasting,
As sure as the morning sun.
He is my double portion,
Source, resource, and supply;
Apart from Him I can do nothing
But wither, shrivel, and die.

I put no trust in carnal weapons
Or in missiles of defense;
I do not trust in flesh and blood
Or any human instruments.
All of my help comes from the Lord;
Through Him my revolutions are won.
And He is the reason why this
Declaration of Dependence was done.

Scriptural reference: Acts 17:28

Be At Home Lord

Be at home Lord…be at home,
In my life Lord…be at home.
Not to visit, but to live in me,
Be at home Lord…be at home.

Yours is the master key
To my every door;
No need to wait for me,
No need to knock anymore.

My home is a far cry
From what You're use to.
I tried fixing and cleaning it up,
But that's something only You can do.

Lord You're going to find
Things that should not be.
Lord please evict them:
Command that they flee.

There's nowhere in me
That's off-limits to You.
Every bedroom, every closet
Is open to Your full view.

Your seat is at the head of my table,
For You are my honored guest.
Let me serve You my "first fruits"
To You I offer my best.

What is mine is Yours;
I'm no longer my own.
Have Thine own way with me;
Lord, be at home.

Scriptural reference: 1 Corinthians 6:19

Habitat for Eternity

Lord, You are my dwelling place,
The homeland of my soul;
From everlasting to everlasting,
My shelter and my stronghold.

I know when this earthen body,
This flesh habitat is destroyed,
I have a habitat for eternity,
Where I will live overjoyed.

Foxes have their foxholes,
And birds have their nests,
But in You is my soul's
Residence, refuge and rest.

The ancient Seven Wonders
Befell by time's wrecking ball.
But in You the "Ancient of Days,"
Only bountiful blessings befall.

Again I will say of You, Lord,
You are my dwelling place,
My habitat for eternity,
Now by faith, then face to face.

Scriptural reference: Psalm 90 & 91

What Shall I Give?

What shall I give
To the Giver of everything,
When the earth is already His,
And all that dwells therein?

I give new songs of thanksgiving;
Of me, I give clear title and claim.
I give worship, praise, glory and honor,
And I bless His holy name.

Bless the Lord, O my soul,
All that's within, I proclaim!
Bless the Lord, O my soul,
Come on and bless His holy name.

With my heart I bless His name;
He is my first love.
I bless His name with my affection,
Focused on things above.

With my walk, I bless Him,
By keeping my integrity.
With my desires I bless His name;
I seek only what He seeks.

Reflecting on all His benefits,
I bless Him with my memory,
For redemption and for healing,
And for His forgiving me.

To add to Him is impossible;
His glory I cannot increase.
Still, my soul brings drops of water,
As gifts to His overflowing sea.

Scriptural reference: Psalm 103: 1-5

Wing and a Prayer

Lord I'm out here
On a "wing and a prayer."
On the wings of faith,
Only a believer would dare.

"Nothing in my hand I bring
Nothing but the cross I bear,"
For it is written, "On Him"
I must cast my total cares.

I'm on my way to the city
Of salvation's heirs,
To inherit the kingdom
Received from Jesus' share.

From below I know it looks like
I am naïve and didn't prepare.
Like I'm out here on nothing,
On substance less visible than air.

But the Air Traffic Controller,
Is safely directing me there.
If you knew what I know,
You would gladly join me here.

I have no bag, bread or money,
I brought nothing to spare.
The Source as my only resource
Is more than sufficient to get me there.

Lord knows I'm out here
On a wing and a prayer,
Out here on my "wings of faith,"
On a believer's prayer.

Scriptural reference: Hebrew 11:1

Lord knows I'm out here, On a wing and a prayer,
Out here on my "wings of faith," On a believer's prayer...

Paving a Road to Hell

Bright and early in the morning,
God said, "Get out of bed.
Go and work in My vineyard."
I went back to sleep instead.

He said, "Time and workers are few,
Reward and harvest are great,
Whatever is right and agreeable to do,
At day's end would be my rate."

I thought, Why get up so soon,
And work "all the livelong day,"
When those who go in late afternoon
Will receive the same rate of pay.

I had every intention of going later.
Setting my alarm clock an hour fast
To arrive by the eleventh hour;
I'd heard last was first and first last.

But my alarm clock did not go off;
It didn't start me on my way;
It did not wake me up on time;
Old man time does not wait or play.

I jumped up and hit the floor running,
Body and worldly cares had to wait.
Out of breath I made it to the vineyard,
But the work was over and it was too late.

Now it was time for my retirement,
Without heaven's stock or pension plan.
My treasures were laid up on Wall Street,
In a house I'd foolishly built on sand.

Lord knows I thought I had time,
Though I had no way to measure or tell.
Unfortunately, all of my good intentions
Were paving a road to hell.

Scripture reference: Matthew 20:1-16

Tell Me…Did You…When I?

I had a dream the other night
That mankind was on trial.
Upon the bench enrobed in glory and might,
The Judge reviewed the evidentiary file.

All the while a soundtrack
In the background could be heard.
A chorus of angelic voices
Singing over and over these words:

"Tell Me, when I was hungry,
Did you give Me something to eat?
When I was sick and imprisoned,
Did you come and see about Me?
When I was cold and naked,
Did you attempt to cover My skin?
When I was sleeping out on the streets,
Did you invite Me in?"

Those to His left cried out,
"Lord how could this be true?
For surely we would have recognized
One as glorious and mighty as You."

"What you did or did not do
To the least among you
Are the things you did to Me,
Are the things that you did not do.
Tell Me when I was hungry,
What gave you Me to eat?
When dusty from My journey,
Did you ever wash My feet?
When I was imprisoned,
Did you come and see about Me?
When I was naked and ashamed,
With Love and clothes did you cover Me?

What you did or did not do
To the least among you
Are the things you did to Me,
Are the things you did not do."

Scriptural reference: Matthew 25:35

Friends in Low Places

I know no people "in the know."
No movers and shakers on the go.
Or those in with the in-crowd,
The high and mighty, or the proud.

But when I stand in need
Of someone to intercede,
I got friends in low places,
With dusty knees and faces.

Friends fervent, tried and true,
Who I can call on or go to,
When the eye of the needle,
I need to get my camels through.

Friends boldly who never cease,
To approach grace's throne seeking mercy,
For me they do intercede,
And grace abounds in my time of need.

As the tallest mountain - Mauna Kea,
Rises from the floor of the sea,
In low places they too stand tallest,
Down on their "bended knee."

I thank God for friends in low places…

Scriptural reference: Hebrew 4:16

I thank God

for friends

in low places...

"Know Jesus, Know Peace"

I searched the whole world over,
Nowhere else could I find
Peace that flowed like a river
That guards my heart and mind.

Peace beyond all understanding,
Yet is no enigma or mystery.
Peace to know that as the day is,
My strength shall equally be.

It may not be trouble-free,
In the midst of storms, safety,
But he never slumbers or sleeps,
For he's watching over me.

Whenever I am disquieted,
I am reminded of this:
For my life there are two choices,
What He ordains and what He permits.

For he is the reason I smile,
In the face of adversity.
It is written, "He's prepared a table
Amidst my enemies for me."

He is the balm for my body and soul,
He fills me with such joy.
A gift more precious than silver and gold,
His righteousness to employ.

Scriptural reference: Isaiah 26:3

The Rich Man and Lazarus

Lord please bring Lazarus
Back to life to be
A warning to my brothers and sisters,
Lest they end up down here with me.

I know they did not listen to Moses,
Nor prophets and preachers you sent.
But perhaps a word delivered by the dead
Will cause them to confess and repent.

Once I was filthy rich and famous,
Living in luxury every day;
My house, my meals and my clothes
Were magnificent in every way.

In my city was a beggar named Lazarus;
Full of sores, he lay outside my gates.
I would not give him the time of day,
Nor the crumbs that fell from my plate.

Lazarus died and went to paradise;
I died and was carted off to hell.
Lazarus was given comfort and delight,
While I received deprivation and travail.

In the afterlife, things turned bottoms up;
Suddenly there was a switch.
I became the one with the beggar's cup,
And Lazarus was abundantly rich.

I beg you, Lord, to have mercy
On me and on my family.
Send Lazarus to witness and to warn them,
Lest they end up down here with me.

I know the living Word forewarned them,
As did the prophets time and again.
But maybe a word delivered by the dead
Will help them avoid the place of torment I'm in.

Scriptural reference: Luke 16:19-31

Keep Oil in Your Lamp

Keep oil in your lamp;
Who knows when the Bridegroom arrives?
Every lamp bearer must carry his own.
You can be foolish, or you can be wise.

Rest assured for He is coming;
Only the Father knows the day.
Keep watch and be also ready,
For Christ is on His way.

At an unsuspecting hour,
We will hear a universal shout,
"Ready or not, here He comes.
Trim your lamps and gather about."

Go ye out to meet Him,
The wedding is about to begin."
Only those with oil in their lamps
Will be allowed to enter in.

Come, people from every nation and soil,
This truth is for all, friend or enemy.
Once He comes, there will be no oil
To borrow, lend, or for free.

Seek Him while He may be found,
For once the wedding begins
The door to the wedding will be closed,
To His bride He must attend.

Your lamp must be trimmed, and burning bright;
Watch and be ready both day and night.
For the Bridegroom will come suddenly,
But only to those bearing the light.

Scriptural reference: Matthew 25:1-13

Nobody but You Lord

Who else but You Lord,
Would take off divinity
And put on the filthy rags
Of haughty humanity?

Who, knowing no sin,
Would become sin,
Put on its likeness
To make righteous men,

Who else but You Lord,
Having one hundred sheep,
And one of them was lost
And the Shepherd would not sleep?

But leave behind
The ninety-nine,
Then rejoice more over
The lost one He finds.

Who else but You, Lord,
The only begotten,
Would claim wretched hordes
As daughters and sons?

For them to become rich,
You became poor,
And no good thing or blessings,
Withhold from their store,
Nobody but You Lord,
Nobody but You.
This is something, Lord,
Only You would do.

And You did it, Lord,
You did it too.
Nobody but You, Lord,
Nobody but You.

Scriptural reference: 2 Corinthians 8:9

Yes and Amen

When Jesus says yes,
No one can say no.
What He closes or opens,
No one can open or close.

When He is for us,
No one can oppose.
When Jesus says yes,
No one can say no.

When He says, "Be still!"
The wind obeys His will;
When He says, "Come forth!"
Even death's grip must yield.

When all is said and done,
He is mightier than our foe;
He is "Alpha" and "Omega,"
And has the last say so.

He left us His promises;
They are "yes" and "amen."
He fulfills every one.
And His truth He will always defend.

Scriptural reference: 2 Corinthians 1:20

Let God Arise

Let God arise,
Let His enemies be scattered.
Let the righteous abide
Under His almighty shadow.

Let God arise,
Let us follow His lead,
Let those who oppose Him
Either perish or flee.

Like wax before the fire
And smoke before the wind,
Like night before the dawn,
They shall come to an end.

Let God be worshipped,
Praised, and magnified;
Let us present our bodies,
As a holy, living sacrifice.

For He is the God of salvation,
Upon the clouds He rides;
Let the righteous rejoice in celebration,
As we let God in us arise.

Scriptural reference: Psalm 68

In Due Season

Kingdom work is well described;
"Go into all the world and preach
The Good News of Jesus Christ,
And do good to all you meet."

As the dewdrops reflect the beam
Of the resplendent sun,
In us should also be seen
Reflections of the most Holy One.

But sometimes in well doing,
The Spirit is willing but the flesh weak.
We get weary in well doing,
Experiencing despair and defeat.

Forgetting "we're co-workers with God,"
From the greatest to the least,
His grace is more than sufficient;
We're strongest when we are weak.

We've come too far to go back now;
Besides, the sand has filled in our tracks.
We must keep our hands upon the Gospel plow,
For God's armor does not cover our backs.

The fruit of gratitude and praise
For a servant is fruitless to expect.
It's a thankless, self-denying work
With a reward, not a paycheck.

Lift up your eyes and look at the fields,
All ripe and white with wheat;
If we faint not and finish the work,
In due season we shall reap.

Scriptural reference: Galatian 6:9

Yesterday, Today, and Forevermore

The more all things change,
The more He remains the same,
Christ today, yesterday and forevermore;
Blessed is His holy name.

Of the countless things He has done,
He can do them again and again,
His mercies are as new every morn,
As they were when time began.

He is as He was,
And will always be;
He still heals, saves, and delivers,
And sets the captives free.

All seasons change,
Friends come and go,
But Jesus Christ is the same,
Yesterday, today and forevermore.

Scriptural reference: Hebrew 13:8

Robbery of The High-Way Kind

Bring your full tithe into My storehouse

Of your treasure, talent and time.

If I did not first give you the dollar,

Then you would not owe me a dime.

Is that asking too much of you?

To give back to Me what is mine?

Well, you do not owe Me a penny

If I did not first give you the dime!

I Am the Lord God Almighty;

Go ahead test Me and see.

Give Me the one and I will bless the nine;

You won't have room enough for the increase.

Is that asking too much of you,

To give back to Me what is Mine?

If you say yes or choose not to,

It's robbery of the High-Way kind.

Scriptural reference: Malachi 3:6-11

God's Favor

Like a moving walkway

Is the favor of God.

Conveying us along life's way,

Still or walking, He guides our heart.

Movement from above is beneath us

Throughout all our days;

It is a gift from God,

As is mercy, love and grace.

Law and Grace

God's Law is like an eternal stairway,

Reaching from earth to heaven.

Only Jesus has climbed every step,

And made it into God's presence.

After Jesus fulfilled the Law,

Like an elevator God gave us grace.

Faith in Jesus is its door;

Go through and you are saved.

He knew we would slip and fall,

As we did on the eternal stairway.

But because of Christ's resurrection,

We'll press on toward the upper way.

Scriptural reference: Ephesians 2:4-8

Can

From the word *can't*,

Jesus Removed the *t*

Now I Can do all things through Him

Without a boundary.

Scriptural reference: Philippians 4:13

God's Word

God's Word

Is like a leveler:

If we keep our bubble

Inside the line,

We can build with confidence,

Knowing it will stand the test of time.

Scriptural reference: 2 Timothy 2:15

God's Math
(Multi-Vide and Add-tract)

God's thoughts are not our thoughts;
His ways are not our ways.
As the heavens are higher than the earth,
His thoughts and ways so are they.

His math is not our math,
To multiply, He often divides.
To add, He may subtract;
He "add-tracts" and "multi-vides."

He divides five thousand stomachs,
Into two fish and five loaves of bread.
And twelve baskets are leftover,
With the multitude completely fed.

With God, less is exceedingly more;
Having too many can lose the fight.
One can pursue one thousand,
And two can put ten thousand to flight.

Whatever the problem or situation,
By His sovereignty,
God's math reveals the right answer,
Which is His will for you and me.

Scriptural reference: Isaiah 55:8

Raise is Within

Raise is within praise,
Raise is within praise;
If you are down, you don't have to stay,
For raise is within your praise.

Praise cause walls to fall,
Wins wars without a fight,
Cools the heat of a fiery furnace,
And makes lions lose their appetite.

God lives in the praise of His people:
In His Spirit, there is liberty.
The captors are made captive,
And the captives are made free.

Deliverance is in our hands,
On the tip of our tongue;
Lift up those hands unto the Lord,
Sing unto Him a brand new song.

"O clap your hands, all ye people,
With the voice of triumph shout."
The more we praise Him,
The more He gives us to shout about.

Praise the Lord, for who He is:
God and God alone.
Praise the Lord, for you are His,
Beloved daughter and son.

Praise the Lord for all He's doing,
Praise Him, for all He's done.
Praise the Lord for all He's going to do,
Praise the Lord everyone.

Scriptural reference: Psalm 150

Reading a Different Book

You'd think we were reading a different book.
You'd think we were reading a different book:
If you didn't take time for a closer look,
You'd think we were reading a different book.

While Satan is fighting throughout,
Christians are fighting within
Over doctrine and traditions
All crafted by mere men.

More concerned about mode of worship
Than the one we are worshipping,
Sometimes you'd never know it's the same God
That we all believe in.

With one word or verse of Scripture,
We start a new church with the same name,
Telling everyone else who dare to differ
They are headed to hell's flame.

We criticize each other;
Reputations we defame.
Had we spoken of Jesus half as much,
The gospel would have been proclaimed.

Hung up by things that mean nothing,
Like the nails that held Him to the cross,
Between these mazes of our making,
The child like gospel has been lost.

Who has divided the Messiah?
What denomination has been crucified?
In whose name did John the Baptist baptize?
Who sits at God's right side?

To unite the body
Through the bond of peace, I submit
The words of the Apostle Paul
In Ephesians 4, verses 1-6.

There is but "one body and one spirit,
One hope, one way, and one call,
One Lord, one faith, and one baptism,
One God, one Father of and over all."

Scriptural reference: Ephesians 4:5 and Matthew 15:3

Well Done

The Son of Man shall come in His glory,
The holy angels all around Him.
He shall gather together all nations;
Like a shepherd, He shall separate them.

On that Final Day,
Standing before God's throne,
When we hear Him say, "Well done."
Will He be commending our hire
Or commanding the fire,
When we hear God say, "Well Done"?

Will He say, "Come, My faithful servant.
You have been faithful over a few"?
Or will He say, "Depart from Me.
You I never knew"?

Scriptural reference: Matthew 25:23

No Seedless Harvest

Whatever you desire
Is what you must first give.
Want mercy?
You must be merciful.
Want forgiveness?
You must first forgive.

Want friends?
You must be friendly.
Want to live?
You must let live.
The fruit is within the seed;
Giving brings forth its yield.

Want others to do unto you?
Then first do unto them.
Pour your all into their cup,
And yours will fill to the brim.

For the fruit is waiting in the seed
To bring forth its yield.
Like the lilies in the valley,
And the wheat across the fields.

Scriptural reference: Proverb 18:24 / Matthew 5:7

Got to Go Through

God never said you wouldn't go through;
He said He'd go through with you.
He'd provide a way of escape
And would come to your rescue.

Safe landings can be expected,
But there is no direct flight.
Though joy comes in the morning,
You have to go through the night.

Of course, there will be turbulence
And wind shears along the way.
Never said it would be turbulent-free,
Or "no stopovers" along the way.

Look forward to a safe landing;
Your pilot is the best.
While others may be anxious,
You can be at rest.

Scriptural reference: 1 Corinthians 10:13
(Dedicated To Sharon Mannery)

Knocking on Heaven's Door

Many who speak of heaven,
Will make it to the door
Only to be asked,
"Have we spoken before?"

Many will be surprised
When it closes forevermore,
For they will be left outside,
Knocking on heaven's door.

In the end times, they will say,
"I confessed You at an early age.
Check the church membership roster;
My name should be on the first page.

"Lord, please reopen the door,
That I might pass through."
"Depart from Me," He will answer.
"I have no record of you."

Many will even plead,
"Lord, I did many wonderful things.
I healed the sick, raised the dead,
And even prophesied in Your name.

Lord, please reopen the door,
And let your servant come through.
"Depart from Me," He shall answer.
"I have no record of you."

Still others will proclaim,
"I came a time or two,
Always on the First Sundays.
I even broke bread and shared wine with you."

"Lord, please reopen the door,
And allow your servant through."
And a voice will answer from the inside,
"I repeat, there is no record of you."

Scriptural reference: Luke 13:25

Chosen People

In days of old, He chose a people;
They did not meet the mark.
So he sent His only begotten son,
And choosing Him would set them apart.

He gives this choice to everyone
Who harkens to His voice.
God has a chosen people.
Those who make Christ their choice.

We are a royal priesthood,
A holy people set apart
To show forth His praises
For calling us out of the dark.

He has called us into His marvelous light
That we might lift up our voice.
God has a chosen people.
Those who make Christ their choice.

Choose ye this day whom you will serve;
Will it be God or man?
But "as for me and my house,"
With Christ we have taken a stand.

Scriptural reference: 1 Peter 2:9

It Wasn't the Nails

It wasn't the nails that
Held Him to the cross.
Had He not remained,
The world would be lost.

The ransom was so high,
Only He could pay the cost.
His love for us kept Him there;
His blood covered our faults.

For God so loved the world,
He gave His only begotten Son.
No greater love had been given
By or to anyone.

He was wounded for our transgressions,
Bruised for our iniquities.
By His stripes, we were healed
As He hung on Calvary.

Willingly He gave His life;
It wasn't taken by Satan or men.
He had the power to lay it down,
And the power to take it up again.

He was lifted up from the earth
In order to save all men.
In victory and might He returned to glory,
Surely He shall return again.

Scriptural references: Isaiah 53:4-5 / 1 Timothy 2:6

Who You're Gonna Listen To?

So many choices and voices,
Don't know who to listen to,
Telling you what you can
And what you cannot do.

Telling you, "It's all over;
There simply is no way through.
If you want to see better days,
Take a look in the rearview.

"You might as well write it off as a loss;
Your enemies far outnumber you.
Nothing seized or ripped off
Can ever be recouped."

You just don't fit the profile,
Wrong size, height and hue."
You'll avoid the mirror,
Afraid what they are saying is true.

But this is what the Lord says,
The One who created you,
"You're fearfully and wondrously made;
From My own image, I fashioned you.

For I know the plans I have,
To prosper and not harm you.
The good work in you I started,
To completion I will see through.

Arise, pursue, and recover;
Look to Me and not the odds.
You might get outmanned,
But never 'out-God'."

Scriptural reference: Jeremiah 29:11

Giving God Back His Breath

Everything you can do after you

Give God back His breath

Are things you can add to the résumé

Of things you did all by yourself.

Scripture reference: Act 17:28

Lightly Salted Christians

We are the only light of the world
And salt of the earth.
Light to lead souls to living water,
And salt to create in them thirst.

If we're not the salt of the earth,
Then we're white sand of the beach;
Of little value or worth
Except under beachgoers' feet.

If we're not the world's candle,
Then we're waxed figures or figurines,
From the candlestick to the mantle
Placed on display just to be seen.

There are seven billion on planet earth,
And Christians are two billion strong.
But the fastest-growing religion
Has increasingly becoming Islam.

Two billion lamps and shakers of salt,
But Baptismal pools go undisturbed.
Empty pews and churches for sale,
Like Nero, we appear unperturbed.

If the earth is getting more depraved,
And the world is getting darker and dim,
It's more a reflection on salt and light
Than it is a reflection on them.

Scriptural reference: Matthew 5:13-14

Creation

Creation

  Is

    Only

      One

        Of

          The

            Creator's

              Creations.

Knocking on Wood

Only once did a-knocking on wood

Ever do me any good.

It was the day Jesus knocked.

I opened the door,

And there he stood.

Scriptural reference: Revelation 3:20

Underground Praise

May your faith in God run as deep

As the faith of an underground spring.

While it's miles from reaching the bed of a creek,

Of the sea it rejoices and sings.

Scriptural reference: Hebrew 11:1

Broken Ripcord

Waiting too late

To call on the Lord

Is like having a parachute

With a broken ripcord.

Scripture reference: Isaiah 55:6

Remount

No one is exempt from hard times;

We must face each trial and battle.

Like breaking a horse never ridden,

We must learn to sit in the saddle.

We'll get kicked, bucked and thrown,

Sustain hurt to our hide and pride.

But get up, dust off, and mount up again,

After which we'll enjoy the ride.

Scriptural reference: James 1:3

Equanimity

All things are not to be understood;

Here, trust in God comes into play.

Accepting the bad along with the good

Is acknowledging He is leading the way.

Scriptural reference: Proverb 3:6

Train Up a Child

Boys will be boys,

And one day men.

Like an oak tree sapling,

Train them young while they'll bend.

Scriptural reference: Proverb 22:6

Believe You Received It

Whatsoever you ask for
When you pray,
Believe you received it
To bring it your way.

According to the law
Of cause and effect,
What you believed
You received, you get.

Say to the mountain,
"Be thou cast into the sea."
Never doubt in your heart
And believe it into reality.

Because what you believe is equal
To whatever you truly expect.
Believe you can or cannot,
And on both counts you will be correct.

Being a believer is not enough
As Mark 11:24 attests:
You must believe you received it
For it to manifest.

Scriptural reference: Mark 11:24

When You Get Old

"When you get old, they throw you away,"
At least so I heard an old lady say.
Just who "they" were, she did not convey,
Only that when you get old, they throw you away.

"I don't get much rest
In this ole rest home.
Though I am old and feeble,
My mind runs on and on."

Clutching a picture of her wedding day,
She said "My man worked his way to an early grave.
He wanted them to have a better life,
It was the price he was willing to pay.

Once I was unable to do things for them,
I found myself in their way.
They swear that this isn't true,
But that's just something they say.

"They say, 'We'll visit once a month;
Twice if it is a holiday.'
Well, it's after Thanksgiving,
And I haven't seen them since May.

'I don't want all their time;
I'd settle for some crumbs.
The only reason they call me now
Is to tell me why they can't come.

"I'd love to go to my church,
But I can't drive to and fro.
Every day it looks more like a hearse
Will take me the next time I go."

Then suddenly she brightened up
As if someone was there,
And began to hum this ole song
And rock in her rocking chair.

"When the storms of life are raging, you stand by me.
Whenever the storms of life are raging, you stand by me,
Whenever I am tossed, like a ship out on the sea,
He who rules the wind and water is standing by me."

Scriptural reference: Matthew 15:3-6 / 1 Timothy 5:4

Father Forgive the Dummy

As a kid, I loved watching *The Ed Sullivan Show*. One of his frequent guests was a ventriloquist named Edgar Bergen. As part of his act, Edgar had a "puppet/dummy" named Charlie McCarthy, a distinguished-looking dummy who wore a top hat, a tuxedo and tie, and a monocle in one eye.

Charlie cracked me up as he sat on Edgar Bergen's lap: He said and did all kind of hilarious and outlandish things. As a little boy, I didn't realize that it was not the "puppet/dummy" doing and saying all of those outlandish things but the puppeteer. One night while watching the show with my grandfather Eli Johnson, he told me that Charlie was just a puppet or dummy that was being used and controlled. It was Edgar Bergen's hand up Charlie's back that caused his arms, legs, and mouth to move. The words coming from his mouth were not his own, but Edgar Bergen's words being projected from Charlie.

He told me to take my eyes off of the puppet and to fix them on the puppeteer. Although it was imperceptible at first, I began to notice minimal movement out of the corner of Edger Bergen's mouth and the slightest twitch in his arm and shoulder. Before long I was able to see more clearly what my grandfather saw and said.

Later in life as I reflected back on this show I learned the message taught in Ephesians 6:12, that "we are not fighting against flesh-and-blood enemies, but against evil rulers and authorities of the unseen world, against mighty powers in this dark world, and against evil spirits in the heavenly places." (NLT) I learned that when the negative or hostile actions of the "Charlie McCarthy's" of this world, do and say unpleasant things to me, I need to first recognize that I'm dealing with a dummy. I need to understand why he/she is a dummy in the first place – the puppeteer is using them! Next, I need to focus on the puppeteer who is the adversary we know as Satan. Then I turn to my sword of the spirit, which is the Word of God. In the Word I learned to "lay aside carnal weapons" and respond to the attacks with "weapons mighty in God for the pulling down of strongholds." (2 Corinthians 10:4 NKJV) I learned to take my eye off of the dummy and keep it on the One who made and pulls all strings, Jesus the Christ. By doing so I am able to focus on the righteousness of the Lord who says, "Vengeance is mine," as I stand my ground under His leadership.

Without excusing the dummy's actions, this helps me develop a "Teflon" heart, where spiteful and injurious things people do and say do not stick with me. I have learned that there are lots of dummies in the world who don't know they are dummies being used and controlled by Satan. It has taught me to say as my Savior said at Calvary; "Father forgive them for they know not what they say and do." Thus, I through the Father forgive the dummy.

Scriptural reference: Ephesian 6:12

...but we know that

when he appears we

shall be like him...

1 John 3:2

Just Like Him

It may yet appear who I shall be,
When God gets through with me,
But this one thing I know:
In my encore,
I shall be just like Him.

Transformed into His image,
From mortal to immortality,
Whatever I shall be
Will be perfect for me,
For I shall be just like Him.

Just like Him in all of His glory,
Just like Him in all of His beauty.
This one thing I know:
In my encore,
I shall be just like Him.

Hollywood material I may not be,
I may never walk the carpeted runway floor,
But this one thing I know:
When He makes me over in my encore,
I shall be just like Him.

The fairest among ten thousand,
Full of love and free,
However He remakes me
Will be perfect for me,
For I shall be just like Him.

Scriptural reference: 1 John 3:2

Trials to a Saint

Trials to a saint
Are like the pruning of a tree
That fruit might come forth
More abundantly.

Pruning causes pain and loss;
It often destroys symmetry.
But trials to a saint
Are like pruning to a tree.

I know it may sound foolish,
To some even lunacy.
Where sin abounds, grace more abounds;
To increase, you must decrease.

But God's ways are not our ways;
His reasons and ours may not agree.
But if you faint not,
There'll be more fruit on your tree.

For He has a stake in the matter;
It's not just about you and me.
In our trials, He is glorified,
Bringing forth fruit from our tree.

His tool is a heavenly device;
It is divine husbandry.
Trials to a saint
Are like the pruning of a tree.

Scriptural reference: John 15:1–8

Psalm 23 (Commentary)

The Lord is my Shepherd

Jehovah is my Shepherd;
I claim Him as my own.
I unashamedly own Him
For me and myself alone.

I shall not want:

No good thing does He withhold,
Whatever my need may be.
I shall not want, for I know
All that is His is for me.

He makes me to lie down in green pastures

I confess, I'm spiritually challenged.
Also Intellectually and visually.
I'm deaf, dumb, and blind to my own interest,
To His pastures He makes me

He leads me beside the still waters

I am afraid of running waters;
On them, I can't walk, float, or swim.
And knowing my straying nature,
By still waters, He leads me by them.

He restores my soul

When I go astray,
He leaves behind the fold.
The joy of His salvation finds me,
And He restores my soul.

He leads me in the paths of righteous for His name's sake

He leads me in the righteous path,
With reins on each side of me,
Not for any goodness of my own,
But for His name's sake and glory.

***Ye though I walk through the valley of the shadow of
death I will fear no evil for thou art with me***

I pass through death's valley,
There "the just shall live and walk by faith,"
For I know shadows cannot appear
Without light's presence in the place.

So I just keep on walking,
No need to change my pace.
I will not run nor be alarmed
Or stand still because I'm afraid.

The shadow of a dog cannot bite,
Nor can the shadow of death do harm.
There's nothing to fear, not even fear itself;
I am safe and secure in His arms.

Thy rod and Thy staff they comfort me

His rod corrects and protects me,
And keeps an account of me.
His staff supports and sustains,
Using human and angelic agencies.

***Thou prepared a table before me in the presence
of mine enemies***

We would not be like our God
If we did not have enemies.
"Friendship with the world,
To our God is enmity."

My mind and body are connected,
When bad news knocks at my door.
I lose sleep and my appetite,
Nauseated down to my core.

But He prepares a table before me
While my enemies behold,
And tells me to make ready
To fill my body and soul.

He anointed my head with oil and my cup runneth over

With the "oil of gladness"
And the joy of the Holy Ghost,
I Am anointed my head with oil;
My cup could contain itself no more.

Surely goodness and mercy shall follow me all the days of my life, and I will dwell in the house of the Lord forever

And though I dearly love the Scriptures,
There's none more treasured by me
Than Psalm 23 and verse 5;
This begins with the word *surely*.

I know God reigns above,
And my Savior has gone on before;
That beneath my feet is Satan,
And inside me is the Holy Ghost forevermore.

Then He seals the covenant with *surely*;
His goodness and mercy trails me
To the secret place of the Most High,
To abide under the shadow of the Almighty.

Scriptural reference: Psalm 23

He anointed
my head
with oil and
my cup
runneth over

About The Author

As President of Faith-Based Communications, **Jerry Mannery** brings a four-fold wealth of experience in music, management, marketing, and ministry. He served as executive director of the gospel division of Malaco/Savoy Music Group for over a decade – overseeing the day-to-day operations of the division, including promotion, production, artist relations, marketing, and administration.

He has served on several music industries Board of Directors, including the Gospel Music Hall of Fame, the American Gospel Quartet Convention, and the Mississippi Musicians Hall of Fame. He is a voting member of The Grammy organization's recording academy (NARAS) and has served as Second Vice-President of the Memphis Chapter, as well as completing a twelve year stint on the Grammy's National Screening Committee for Gospel Music.

Jerry is the founder of the Mississippi Children's Choir, and is a founding member of the Mississippi Mass Choir, where he serves as executive director, and as one of its composers and producers. He has booked and managed tours throughout the country and around the world, including Japan, Spain, Italy, South Africa, Greece, and the Canary Islands.

In 1968, he was one of the first African-American students to integrate the then all white Florence High School.

In 1995, he became the first African-American to retire from the Jackson, Mississippi Fire Department with the rank of captain. He was named Fireman of the Year in 1991 and 1994. In 1996 he was named National Alumnus of the Year at Lanier High School.

A prolific and diverse songwriter, he has written over one hundred songs - recorded by legendary R&B, Blues and Gospel artist. In 2003 he received The Gospel Music Workshop of America Founder's Award, named in honor of the convention founder, Rev. James Cleveland.

For five years he served as Client Service Director for OwensMorris Communications, Inc. - a full service marketing communications agency, with corporate and entertainment clients including TV One, and ExxonMobil. In 2011, he and long time friend Hoyett Owens founded Faith-Based Communications; a full service marketing and communication agency, dedicated to helping their clients reach and influence the faith based market. This company currently manages and produces the McDonald's Inspiration Celebration Gospel Tour.

Notwithstanding all of the aforementioned achievements, his crowning moment came in 2000 when he accepted his call to the ministry and received his ordination from More than Conquerors Faith Church, of Birmingham, Alabama, and North Star M.B. Church of Lake Providence, Louisian.

He and his wife of thirty-five years, Sharon, have two children- Dr. Yanci Olivia Baker (Benjamin) and Jerron Eli Mannery (Kassundra). They have four adorable grandchildren – Kennedi, Landon, Ansleigh, and Olivia.

About the Illustrator

Tracy Applewhite Broome met Jerry over 20 years ago when she pursued her dream as a graphic artist to design album covers for the Mississippi Mass Choir. Jerry became more than a business contact, he became a lifelong source of friendship and encouragement from the moment she talked to him.

Tracy is an artist and lives on the beautiful Mississippi Gulf Coast with her family. She enjoys working with inspirational authors such as Jerry Mannery. She is passionate about painting images that communicate hope and happiness and her desire is to point people to the Master Creator through her art.

About The Editor

John Milton Wesley

Place of residence: Ellicott City, Maryland

Birthplace: Ruleville, Mississippi

Grew up in the Mississippi Delta. Moved to Jackson on June 12, 1963, the night Medgar Evers was gunned down in his driveway.

Day job: Partnership development, marketing, media and idea development, and consultant.

Education: Tougaloo College, Mississippi. Yale University. Columbia University Graduate School of Journalism

Anthologies: Black Southern Voices. Mississippi Writers, Volume III

Serial publications: Essence Magazine. Prevention. Pipeland Magazine

Awards: Reader's Digest United Negro College Fund First Place Award for Poetry, 1968. Maryland Department of Health and Mental Hygiene Outstanding Community Service Award, 1988. National Conference of Blacks in Government

Current project: Novel and screenplay set in 1957 Mississippi

Favorite book: Living Well is the Best Revenge by Calvin Tomkins

Belief: Despite your fame, weather will determine the attendance at your funeral.

Lightning Source UK Ltd.
Milton Keynes UK
UKOW07f2334270217
295497UK00010B/69/P